Timeline of the Fire of London

4th September 1666

The fire has spread far and wide, destroying important buildings such as St Paul's Cathedral, but stops halfway across London Bridge.

Summer 1666

London is hot and bone-dry after 10 months of drought.

5th September 1666

The fire begins to die down when the strong east wind drops and men led by the Duke of York demolish the buildings in its path.

2nd September 1666

A fire breaks out in Tom Farynor's bakery in the heart of the city when he forgets to completely extinguish the oven.

6th September 1666

The last large fires are extinguished in the night, but small fires will linger for weeks.

1667

People clear away the rubble and inspect the burnt area. New laws are passed on how houses should be built. But by the end of the year only 150 new houses are finished.

1677

The monument designed by Sir Christopher Wren to commemorate the Great Fire of London is finished. It still stands today.

Winter 1666

The fields around London are filled with homeless people who are forced to live in tents after losing their homes in the fire.

1672

By now around 9,000 houses are rebuilt, most in brick instead of wood. Streets are widened and new ones are created. Pavements are built for the first time and new sewers are added. Most of those who lost houses now have new homes.

Map of London after the 1666 Fire

After the Great Fire had been extinguished, plans for the rebuilding of London were drawn up by the architect Sir Christopher Wren, writer John Evelyn, and scientist Robert Hooke. These plans were very ambitious. Wren wished to build much wider streets than before, outlining three standard widths of thirty, sixty and ninety feet (9, 18 and 27 metres).

Although these plans were never carried out, the new city was very different to the old one. Rich aristocrats decided to move into new houses in the West End, creating fashionable districts such as St James'. The divide between the middle-class City of London, where merchants lived, and the aristocratic court in Westminster, became much more obvious.

Author:
Jim Pipe studied Ancient & Modern History at Oxford University, then spent ten years in publishing before becoming a full-time writer. He has written numerous non-fiction books for children, many on historical subjects. He lives in Dublin, Ireland, with his lovely wife Melissa and twin boys Daniel and Ewan.

Artist:
David Antram was born in Brighton, England, in 1958. He studied at Eastbourne College of Art and then worked in advertising for fifteen years before becoming a full-time artist. He has illustrated many children's non-fiction books.

Series creator:
David Salariya was born in Dundee, Scotland. He has illustrated a wide range of books and has created and designed many new series for publishers in the UK and overseas. David established The Salariya Book Company in 1989. He lives in Brighton, England, with his wife, illustrator Shirley Willis, and their son Jonathan.

Editor: **Stephen Haynes**

Editorial Assistants: **Mark Williams, Tanya Kant**

Published in Great Britain in MMXVI by
Book House, an imprint of
The Salariya Book Company Ltd
25 Marlborough Place, Brighton BN1 1UB
www.salariya.com
ISBN: 978-1-910706-43-5

SCRIBO   BOOK HOUSE   SCRIBBLERS

5 7 9 8 6

A CIP catalogue record for this book is available from the British Library.

Printed and bound in China.
Printed on paper from sustainable sources.
Reprinted in MMXIX.

Visit
www.salariya.com
for our online catalogue and **free** fun stuff.

PAPER FROM
SUSTAINABLE
FORESTS

You Wouldn't Want to Be® in the Great Fire of London!

Written by
Jim Pipe

Illustrated by
David Antram

Created and designed by
David Salariya

A Fire You'd Rather Not Fight

BOOK HOUSE
a SALARIYA *imprint*

Contents

Introduction

You are Samuel Pepys (say 'peeps'), born in 1633 and the fifth of eleven children. You're the son of a humble tailor, but through hard work and talent – and help from a rich relative, Sir Edward Montagu – you become Clerk for the Royal Navy for King Charles II of England.

Around 1660, you begin keeping a secret diary, little knowing what horrors lie ahead. In 1665, London is devastated by a deadly plague that kills 100,000 people. Then, in the early hours of 2 September 1666, a fire breaks out in a bakery in the heart of the City. The blaze spreads rapidly. Like everyone else, you're terrified your house and belongings will be destroyed. What can you do to stop the fire spreading, especially when the streets are packed with Londoners desperate to escape the inferno?

The Great Fire of London raged for four nights and days. Most of medieval London was burnt to the ground.

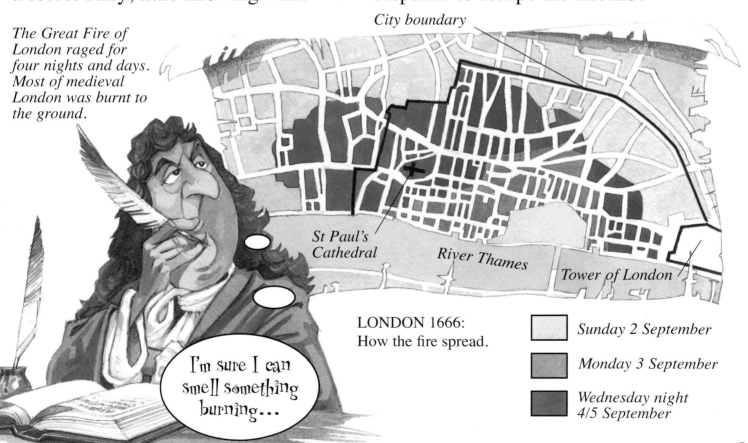

City boundary

St Paul's Cathedral

River Thames

Tower of London

LONDON 1666:
How the fire spread.

Sunday 2 September

Monday 3 September

Wednesday night 4/5 September

I'm sure I can smell something burning…

Dirty old town

Strolling through London in the summer of 1666, it's easy to be swamped by the sights, sounds and smells of this busy metropolis. London is a giant city with over 300,000 inhabitants. It's also a centre for trade, finance and government, a wealthy place where lords are carried in grand coaches by servants.

Yet the old centre of London, the City, is a horrible place. Its smoky streets are narrow, stuffy and dark. The summer of 1666 is hot and the place is bone-dry after 10 months of drought. You hold your nose to avoid the stench of dead dogs and rotting waste.

Mustn't smile, mustn't smile...

I feel much better, honest!

Why is life so grim?

IN THE NOISY STREETS, shouting matches are common. There are no street signs so you find your way around by shop signs. A sign showing a dragon marks an apothecary's (chemist's), and Adam and Eve mark a fruit shop.

FASHION. Women wear hideous white make-up made from poisonous lead. It smells foul and cracks when they smile. People use small bits of mouse skin to make their eyebrows look stylish!

WIGS. Charles II begins wearing wigs when he sees his first grey hairs. Most men copy him. Nits and lice are common problems.

MEDICINE is basic. Hospitals are a place to rest, but little else. Doctors cure their patients using leeches to suck their blood.

POLLUTION. Ashes and dust are constantly thrown into the streets. Piles of steaming dung lie everywhere. Every home has a cesspit for sewage. In your diary you moan that your neighbour's cesspit has flooded your cellar.

Troubled times

I t isn't just the hot weather that bothers you. England is still recovering from a bloody civil war fought between Parliament and King Charles I. In 1660, King Charles II was restored to the throne, but old rivalries remain.

A year ago, a third of Londoners died during a horrific plague. The churchyards were full of bodies piled on top of each other. The plague has almost died out now, but death carts still rattle around the streets. To make matters worse, England is at war with the Netherlands, and there is tension between Protestants and Catholics.

Even in 21st-century London, it is said that you are never more than 2 metres away from a rat!

Where are we going to bury them all?

Why are people so fearful?

PLAGUE. In September 1665, the plague killed 8,000 Londoners in a single week. In October, the disease died down, as cold weather killed rats carrying the infected fleas that cause the disease. But 100,000 Londoners were already dead.

TENSION. London is a largely Protestant place. In 1605 a group of Catholics led by Guy Fawkes tried to blow up Parliament – the Gunpowder Plot. Protestants now fear another Catholic plot to destroy the city.

WAR. In recent times England has been at war with Spain and France and in September 1666 it is fighting the Dutch. Londoners are suspicious of foreigners, especially the French, as they fear a French invasion.

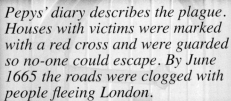

Pepys' diary describes the plague. Houses with victims were marked with a red cross and were guarded so no-one could escape. By June 1665 the roads were clogged with people fleeing London.

Never trust a man with a French hat!

FLOODED & FROZEN. In 1663, high tide flooded central London. The River Thames also froze over for several winters in the 1660s. At the best of times, the river is full of floating corpses and waste. At low tide it stinks horribly.

A bonfire waiting to happen?

As if Londoners don't already have enough worries, fires are common. A fire in 1633 burnt for 8 hours and wrecked over 80 houses. Despite this, open fires burn in houses, shops and workshops. Craftsmen light braziers in the streets. The houses crowded inside the City walls are built of timber. Straw is laid on floors and stored in stables, so a careless neighbour can soon start a mighty blaze.

You've heard all sorts of predictions that London will burn down. Being a superstitious chap, you wear a hare's foot around your neck as a good-luck charm. Terrifyingly, your worst fears are about to come true.

People cook and heat their houses with open fire and use candles in the dark. Some smoke in bed or sweep hot ashes under the stairs.

Who predicts the Great Fire?

IN APRIL 1665, Charles II warns the Lord Mayor of the fire risks of the City's wooden houses and narrow streets. From 1600 to 1665 there have been at least 70 big fires in English towns.

SUPERSTITIOUS PEOPLE believe they see signs of disaster. At Easter it rains fish in Kent. In July, egg-sized hailstones fall in Norfolk. Months before the fire, the Spanish ambassador says he sees a monster 'with a human face, the legs of a bull, the tail of a wolf and the breast of a goat'.

Fire hazard!

- Clothes hung too close to a fire can easily catch alight.

- Some people believe that smoking wards off the plague, so fires are a big risk.

- Barrels of cooking oil kept in a cellar can create a raging inferno if they catch fire.

- In 1649, 27 barrels of gunpowder stored in a cellar blew up, destroying 41 houses and killing 67 people.

RELIGIOUS PAMPHLETS have been warning of a great fire for years. They say that God is going to send fire to punish Londoners for their sins. You're afraid bad things may happen in 1666 because 666 is the symbol of the devil.

IN A BOOK written in 1641, Mother Shipton, a so-called witch from York, predicts that 'London in '66 should be burnt to ashes'. People take such warnings very seriously.

May the fires of hell rain down on London!

Mother Shipton says things are hotting up!

15

The fire begins

Saturday 1 September is another hot, dry day. Trade is busy and by closing time, baker Tom Farynor is exhausted. When he cools the ovens, he misses a glowing ember.

While you are sleeping in the early hours of Sunday 2 September, a small fire starts in Farynor's bakery on Pudding Lane. It is fanned by the easterly breeze blowing across the city. The fire spreads quickly through the house. Soon after 2 a.m., Farynor's assistant is woken by thick smoke. He raises the alarm and Farynor and his family escape through an attic window to a neighbour's house – all except a maid, who is scared of heights and stays behind. She is the fire's first victim.

How does the fire spread?

1. FARYNOR'S BAKERY. As Farynor's bakery burns, a group from the nearby Star Inn stand and gawp, rather than trying to put out the fire.

Farynor's neighbour even has time to remove his goods before the fire spreads to his house. Then, without warning, the roof of the bakery suddenly collapses.

2. STAR INN. Sparks blow across the yard to the Star Inn, which instantly catches fire. The flames are soon roaring. People living in Pudding Lane and Fish Street Hill pour onto the streets to put out the flames.

Handy hint

Take the fire seriously! When the Lord Mayor is woken and told of the fire, he says: 'Pish, a woman could put the fire out by peeing on it!' and goes back to bed.

4. THE RIVERSIDE WAREHOUSES are packed with oil, pitch, hay, coal, hemp and tar. These fuel the fire, which burns so fiercely that no-one can get close enough to fight the flames.

5. THE CITY. The strong wind spreads the flames into the City. By 8 a.m., the blaze has spread halfway across London Bridge, destroying the houses that are built on the bridge itself. Luckily, a gap in the houses created by the fire of 1633 stops it spreading across the river.

Pudding Lane

Fish Street Hill

London Bridge

Thames Street

It's hotter than the devil's underwear.

The yellow area (above) shows how far the fire spread on Sunday 2 September

3. THAMES STREET. Sparks carried by the strong east wind set alight wooden houses up to 200 metres away. Timber beams fall across the streets and provide another route for the fire. Towards dawn, the fire spreads to St Botolph's Lane and down Fish Street Hill to the warehouses on Thames Street.

17

The blaze spreads

A couple of hours after the blaze starts, your maid wakes you to warn of the danger. Seeing the fire is some way off, you head back to bed. She bursts in later with news that 300 buildings are already in ashes. This is no ordinary blaze. You hurry to the top of the Tower of London to see for yourself. Getting into a boat, you watch burning timbers fall into the water – the river itself seems on fire! The blaze is spreading west at great speed, whipped along by the wind. Around 11 a.m., you travel to Whitehall to tell the King.

How do people react?

WHAT FIRE? It's a while before people realise the danger. Swedish diplomat Francisco de Rapicani describes having lunch out with friends. They return home to find 'their houses have gone up in fire and smoke'!

HOLDING OUT. People stay in their homes as long as they can. You see pigeons unwilling to leave their nests, hovering above the flaming roofs until their wings burn and they fall into the fire.

FIREBREAKS. By the time the Lord Mayor arrives, the fire has spread to the river. One way of stopping it is to create firebreaks by pulling down houses in its path. But when the owners refuse to let him demolish their homes, the Mayor hesitates. Quick action could have stopped the fire from spreading.

Forget it!

Please! Let me pull down your house!

Everything will burn, even the churches! I must tell the king!*

Handy hint

If you're making a run for it, don't forget your pet! Later in the week you see a shivering cat. Its fur has been burnt off by the flames but it is still alive.

PANIC. By now everyone is fleeing, pushing their way through narrow streets. People and horses are running over each other! It's very hard to get water pumps (see page 16) to the fire quickly.

He's got a firebomb!

It's just a tennis ball!

ANGER. On the way to see the King, you meet an angry crowd who believe God has sent the fire. There's also a rumour that foreigners are throwing fireballs to start the fires. Mobs, armed with clubs and home-made weapons, attack anyone who can't speak good English.

* Despite what Pepys had seen, he still had a dinner party for his friends that night!

Battling the inferno

When you tell the King the bad news, he leaps into action. A coach takes you to the Lord Mayor with orders that no houses are to be spared in putting out the fire. By noon a few firebreaks have been created, but they're too close to the fire to stop it. That afternoon, the King lends a hand to the people fighting the fire. By now the flames are shooting 30 metres into the air. Later that night, you watch from the river. Your face is burned by a shower of 'fire drops'.

How can the fire be stopped?

That's more like it!

I'm too tired to care! I need more men!

FIRE BRIGADE? There isn't one. Locals fight the flames with water carried in leather buckets or by beating the fire out. The authorities have a few hand-pumped machines that squirt water, but they won't stop fast-moving fires.

Water pump

ASK THE MAYOR? Don't bother. When you finally deliver the King's message to the Lord Mayor he drops to his knees, whimpering.

20

On Tuesday night, soldiers and sailors use gunpowder to knock down houses, which proves far more effective.

BOOM!

Handy hint

By Sunday evening the fire is so strong it's moving against the wind – toward your house! Go home and pack up your belongings!

Those wigs must be soundproofed!

PULL HOMES DOWN? Where fires threaten to spread, people use axes, ropes and iron fire hooks to drag down buildings and create firebreaks. But the wind sweeps the fire so fast that the houses can't be pulled down quickly enough. At its peak, the blaze wrecks about 100 houses an hour.

HEAVE!

Uh-oh!

WATER PUMPS? There's a system of wooden water pipes below ground to feed the pumps during fires. In the rush to stop the fire, people tear up the streets, piercing the pipes in so many places that there is no pressure to squirt the water out.

21

A lake of fire

How can you save your belongings?

At 4 a.m. the next day, Monday, you move your silver and valuables to a friend's house outside the City walls. You're in such a rush you don't change out of your nightgown!

Meanwhile, the Royal Exchange building, packed with expensive silks and spices, goes up in flames. The smoke turns the sky red.

On Tuesday, the fire moves west and north. After midnight, it destroys the Guildhall and St Paul's Cathedral. Lead melted from buildings runs down streets that are glowing with the heat. Around 2 a.m. on Wednesday your wife wakes you. The fire is perilously close to your house. You decide to escape by boat.

BY RIVER. You pay £8 for two boats to carry your furniture downriver to Deptford. Other people flee in 'wherries' – small river boats. You see a few boats carrying virginals (musical instruments). The Thames is littered with abandoned goods.

BY CART. When the river boats are filled with refugees, there's only one way for people to move their things – by cart. The price of a cart rises from £3 to £30 in two days. One desperate man even pays £400 (around £40,000 today).

ON FOOT. Some people can't afford boats, so they carry what they can. Sick and elderly people will need a helping hand. With London Bridge in flames there's no way across the river except by boat. Few people know how to swim.

UNDERGROUND. People with valuables bury or hide them underground before fleeing. On Tuesday you bury your prized Parmesan cheeses and wine stores. You also place some important documents in your neighbour's pit.

£400?

It's my hottest price!

Pepys wrote in his diary that the night sky was lit 'as if the whole heaven was on fire'.

I'm glad we left the kitchen sink behind.

23

The fire dies down

The fire rages for four nights and days. You see houses in the east being blown up by gunpowder, which creates large firebreaks and saves the Tower of London. But in the west, the fire leaps across the Fleet River and threatens Whitehall and the royal palaces.

Finally, on Wednesday morning, the wind drops. The fire slowly begins to burn out. At last people can put out the flames, though they battle for another 36 hours before the last fires are extinguished on Thursday night. Earlier that day you walk around the smoking ruins of the City. Small fires smoulder for many weeks after.

Pepys was very sad to see the smoking ruins of St Paul's Cathedral.

Why did the fire stop?

WIND. The east wind fanned the fire. When it dropped the flames died down.

STONE WALLS. The Temple is an ancient medieval church surrounded by stone buildings belonging to lawyers. Finally the fire had come up against buildings it couldn't burn.

DEMOLITION. On Monday the King asked the Duke of York (the future James II) to take charge. The Duke organised a series of explosions that stopped the fire.

What about the survivors?

OVER 100,000 Londoners have had to flee their homes. Many go to the suburbs and stay there. Some go to other towns, while others emigrate to America. In the winter of 1666, the fields around London are full of the homeless living in tents.

Navy biscuit – hard biscuits used by the Navy – is handed out but many people refuse it.

Handy hint

Watch out for sudden flare-ups. Fires smouldering in cellars keep breaking out up to six months after the Great Fire.

Is it safe to come out now?

SHACKED UP. Some Londoners set up shacks made from charred wood and fallen bricks over the smoking rubble. This is brave but very dangerous. At night many people are robbed, murdered and then buried in the ruins.

ROASTED. Not everyone was able to escape the flames. Londoner Thomas Taswell describes his horror at finding the gruesome remains of an old woman burnt in the fire.

A city in ruins

You're incredibly lucky – the fire stops at the end of your street, Seething Lane, and your house is untouched. Because your house is a government building, you persuaded the Duke of York to create firebreaks nearby to protect your street! But all around there is devastation. The Great Fire is one of the greatest disasters in London's history. Thousands of people have lost their homes, businesses and belongings.

News of the Great Fire quickly spreads around Europe and foreign newspapers print the story with dramatic drawings of the fire.

DESTRUCTION. The Great Fire has destroyed 13,200 houses and four-fifths of the City of London, including the Royal Exchange and the Custom House. As well as St Paul's Cathedral, 87 churches are destroyed.

St Paul's Cathedral

River Thames

LOST LIVES. The Great Fire starts slowly, so there is plenty of time for people to save themselves. Officially, there are just six deaths: Thomas Farynor's maid; Paul Lowell, a watchmaker; an old man who was overcome by smoke; an unnamed old woman found near St Paul's; and two bodies inside the cathedral. However, it is likely there were many more unrecorded victims.

BANKRUPTCY. So many merchants are ruined that a new prison is built for those who can't pay their debts. Others kill themselves. After the fire, Sarah Crofts, once a wealthy woman, has to work as a servant after losing property worth £5,000.

Handy hint
Even if your house is burnt, check your cellar for any goods that aren't ruined. The Grocers' Company found 100 kg of silver from coins that had melted in the heat!

Tower of London

Royal Exchange

Southwark

London Bridge

Aftermath

The Great Fire is a disaster but it does bring change. Many of the new houses are built in brick and stone. A huge army of migrant workers come to rebuild the city, along with craftsmen to furnish the new houses. By the early 18th century, London is the largest city in Europe and probably the richest. It also has some wonderful new buildings, such as St Paul's.

Though houses built after the Great Fire are safer, a large fire in 1676 destroys over 600 houses south of the river. In January 1673, a fire destroys your home. Eleven years later another home of yours is only saved when a neighbour's house is blown up to create a firebreak. Will you ever be able to sleep in peace?

Better firefighting

INSURANCE. There is no home insurance so Londoners have to pay for their burnt houses to be rebuilt. This is such a problem that in 1680 Nicholas Barbon sets up the first insurance company, called The Fire Office. However, London doesn't have a proper fire brigade until 1866.

A NEW LAW passed in 1668 requires Londoners to keep a better look-out for fires. Large numbers of buckets, ladders and pick-axes are kept at the ready.

Oh, not again!

32

FIRE ENGINE. In the 1670s, Dutch inventor Jan van der Heyden invents a new fire engine with a leather hose known as a 'worm' or 'snake'. It also has an air pump that creates a continuous stream of water. The fire engine is first used in London in the 1690s.

The Monument

Handy hint

Look out for the yellow flowers of wild mustard that grow over the wastelands created by the fire. The flowers spread so fast that they are nicknamed 'London rocket'!

What survives today?

BURNT. Very few buildings from before the fire still stand today, though some survived into the 19th century.

THE GEORGE

St Paul's Cathedral

THE MONUMENT. Designed by Wren and Hooke, this column (right) marks the Great Fire. It stands near Pudding Lane, close to where the fire started. It's 62 m tall. You can still climb the column's 311 interior steps to enjoy the view from the top.

ST PAUL'S CATHEDRAL. The most famous building designed by Wren, the new cathedral was built from 1675 to 1710. Twenty-nine of the other 51 churches designed by Wren are still standing.

Glossary

Apothecary A historical name for a chemist or pharmacist.

Bankrupt Having no money and unable to pay one's debts.

Brazier A large metal container in which coal or charcoal was burned, used to warm people.

Cesspit A large pit dug into the ground, used to collect sewage or rubbish in the days before towns had sewers.

Chamber pot A bowl-shaped pot with a handle, kept in the bedroom under a bed or in a cabinet, used for going to the toilet in the night. Also known as a bedpan.

Civil War The war fought between the supporters of Parliament, led by Oliver Cromwell, and King Charles I. It lasted from 1641 to 1651. It ended with the Parliamentary victory at the Battle of Worcester on 3 September 1651.

Clerk Pepys' full title was Clerk of the Acts. He was responsible for organising supplies for the Royal Navy.

Coal tax After the Great Fire of London, Parliament introduced a tax on coal which it used to rebuild the city.

Courtier Someone who attends the court of a king or queen. In the past, the court was a centre of power and courtiers who flattered the king might be rewarded with money, land or titles.

Drought A long dry spell of weather, often leading to a shortage of water.

Ember A hot fragment of wood or coal left from a fire that is still glowing or smouldering.

Fireball A ball of animal fat, called tallow, set alight and used to start fires.

Firebreak A gap between houses that stops a fire from spreading. During the Great Fire, firebreaks were created by pulling down houses or blowing them up.

Fire Court A special court set up after the Great Fire to settle arguments between landlords and tenants.

Hemp A fibre made from the hemp plant that was used in the past to make ropes and nets.

Inquiry An official investigation.

Insurance An agreement that protects against a future loss. For example, if you insure a house and it burns down, you will be paid the money to rebuild it.

King's Council A group of ministers who helped advise the king.

Leech A bloodsucking worm-like creature that often lives in water. In the past, leeches were used to draw blood from patients as a supposed cure for many different illnesses and diseases.

Lord Mayor The elected head of the City of London's governing body.

Metropolis A large and heavily populated city, such as London.

Migrant Someone who comes to live in a different country.

Navy biscuit A hard biscuit made of flour, salt and water used by the Royal Navy to feed crews on long sea voyages.

Parliament The government of England which passes new laws.

Pitch A black, sticky substance, also known as tar, that is used to stop wooden ships from leaking.

Plague A deadly disease spread quickly by fleas.

River Fleet A small river that flows south into the River Thames in London.

Smoulder To burn without a flame.

Suburb A district lying in the outer parts of a city.

Warehouse A store for goods and merchandise.

Wherry A small boat used to transport goods along a river.

Index

The Monument by Sir Christopher Wren

Sir Christopher Wren, Surveyor General to King Charles II and architect of St Paul's Cathedral, and his colleague, Dr Robert Hooke, were tasked with designing a permanent memorial to the Great Fire of London. It was to be erected near Pudding Lane where the fire began.

Their design is a Doric column 61 metres high – the distance between it and the site in Pudding Lane where the fire started – with a staircase inside leading up to a viewing platform at the top. A drum and a copper urn decorated with flames, symbolising the fire, sits at the very top of the structure.

When the column was completed in 1677, it was initially used as a location where the Royal Society could carry out experiments, but traffic vibrations interfered with these. Since then, it has remained as a tourist attraction.

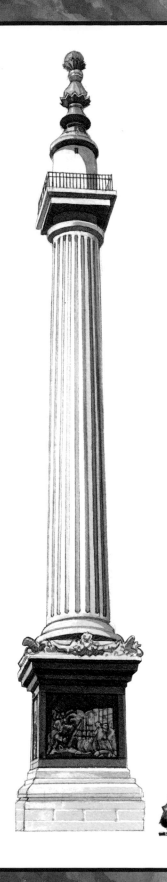

Other London disasters

Plagues In 1348, the Black Death wiped out half of London's population. In Tudor times, a mysterious 'sweating sickness' struck at least six times and in 1528 polished off several thousand people in just a few hours. Cholera and typhoid were common until the rebuilding of London's sewers in Victorian times.

Floods In 1579 the river Thames rose so high that fish were left stranded in Westminster Hall! As recently as 1953, deadly floods swept much of south-east England, including London.

Storms In 1090, 600 houses were blown down by a great wind. A hurricane in 1703 blew lead roofing off Westminster Abbey; Queen Anne had to shelter in a cellar at St James's Palace. Bizarrely, sand from the Sahara desert fell on Morden in south London in the same year.

Earthquakes Yes, really! Quakes were recorded in 1247, 1275, 1382, 1439, 1626 and 1750. The actor Richard Tarleton watched in 1580 as two men sitting on a cannon at Tower Hill were thrown off by a tremor, which also set the city's bells ringing. Don't be too worried – only one Londoner has ever been killed by an earthquake: cobbler Thomas Grey was crushed by falling bricks in Newgate Street in the earthquake of 1580.

Tornado In December 2006 a tornado ripped through Kensal Green, injuring six people and damaging over 100 properties.

Shipwrecks In 1878, 600 people died when the SS Princess Alice sank after a collision with another boat near Woolwich. The passengers were either trapped in the sinking vessel or thrown into the heavily polluted river – a rather grim end.

Fog and smog Charles Dickens called the fog 'London's ivy', as it clung to everything. In the Victorian era, half a million coal fires helped to create the phenomenon known as a 'London particular' or 'pea-souper'. Fog caused 700 deaths in 1873, including 19 people who walked into the river, docks or canals. French painter Claude Monet visited London in 1899 and 1901 just to paint the fogs!